A Full Cup OF NosEEy Me

Fruity Birdbrain Behind Bars

Nita Hampton

Published and Distributed By
S. Hampton Foundation Publishing
Los Angeles, California
Email: smhampton1976@gmail.com

Packaging/Consulting
Professional Publishing House
1425 W. Manchester Ave. Ste B
Los Angeles, California 90047
323-750-3592
Email: professionalpublishinghouse@yahoo.com
www.Professionalpublishinghouse.com

Cover design and artwork by Shanita Hampton
First printing July 2021
978-1-7368493-0-9
10987654321

Special Thanks...

To a great son, Christopher.

Son, you have inspired me to look beyond the skin when you said, "Mom, why don't you look a little deeper?" I took your words, along with your happy energy off with me. Now this life journey means so much more to me.

Son, you are the reason I now believe in our family tree. I love all my family.

As I looked within myself, a rosebud was shown to me. The bud pinned up with emotions, alone with nothing to offer. Only to realize in due time the bud of the brain would blossom, refreshing the entire globe.

Dedications...

I dedicate this book to my family,. Margie (mother), Laqueta (sister), Maurice (brother), Kendra (sister), Daylan (brother), Marcella (sister), Starrla (sister), Tanesha (sister), with so many more family members to name. Thank you all.

Acknowledgments...

I want to thank the one and only Coach Ron, who always wanted the best for us.

Thanks to Brother Bryant for Pasadena Youth Christian Center.

Positivity over negativity is God's good energy.

Introduction...

A Full Cup of NosEEy Me is based on a true story. All my life I had my hand up asking questions. The need to know why, wouldn't let me sleep. Nosey people don't sit around, their wheels keep spinning round. The entire world happens to be my playground. Plenty rings of fire, but my heart had only one desire...Truth.

Fruity Birdbrain
Behind Bars

I started going to jail as soon as my eighteenth birthday hit. I remember chilling with this dude at my house. Asia sat on the couch and I sat on his lap, as if I was riding a horse. He was one of those mixed dudes. I thought he was kind of cute, with his Steve Harvey haircut. Those were in style. Heck, they looked good to me. Well, we heard someone at the door, and lo and behold, it was the damn police. I had the screen door closed but the wooden door was open, so they came right on in. We jumped up, he grabbed his pants, and I tried to rush to the bathroom. I knew they were looking for whoever lived in this joint and had the drugs.

I didn't get far. Someone tossed me to the floor, and put their knee in my back, quicker than a midget hitting the ground. We ended up sitting there until they searched the whole house. Oh, here we go. They found crap everywhere, even in the bottom of the baby's bed. Good thing no baby lived there or I would have been in some deep boo-boo. They started with their routine questioning: "Who lived here? Whose house is this? Is this your crack? Is this your leafy looking stuff?" Of course the dude was just visiting, so he was like, "That's not mine, and I don't live here. I don't even know what that crap is that you're speaking on." They took him

in the restroom, and searched him. They wanted to see if he was telling the truth, or if he had anything on him. This was one of those good mixed dudes. I guess I know how to pick them.

Since he told the truth they let him sit on the couch. As for me, I lived there with my uncle, who had traffic in and out the house. This was why the police came in the first place. Heck, I can't lie, the money seemed easy to get. So, when he was away I figured, "Why not make a little cash? We all need money to survive, and have fun." The green leafy stuff they found was mine. Shoot, I smoked so much of what I sold, that I didn't even remember any of the places I stashed my supply. Guess what? They had no problem finding it all. I had a feeling I would be going to jail for the first time in my life. I went down. It wasn't because I went out and committed a crime; it was because I was at the wrong place at the wrong time. Oh, but did I tell you that I had went to church, so I did understand right from wrong? I couldn't blame anyone but myself.

The police took Asia and I to the same patrol car, sitting side by side, which was nice because, at this point and time, I felt like this night couldn't get worse. I knew they were going to let my little pretty boy go. I asked him if he could hold all my money until I was released from jail, they searched me, but not as well as they should have. I had drugs on me, and about five hundred dollars. I gave it all to my lover boy. This was my first bid. The courts slapped me on the wrist with some county time and probation.

Let me tell you, I thought I was tough until I stepped foot in that awful cell. I was scared. I started my period that very night, but didn't find out until the morning. I went to get up to use the restroom, and there was blood all over my dress and sheets. There was no way a scared girl like me was about to get up in front of all those women. So, I lied there until nighttime, when everyone went to bed, and I crept up to the officers' booth to ask them for some new clothes and pads. Thank God I only had to do a week. I was released and everything was good with ol' boy Asia.

I knew I had to get my life together. I couldn't live at the same spot. I had just graduated and needed somewhere to go in order to get my thoughts together. I had to get back on track with my schooling. I ended up back at my mom's house and headed to a community college. The neighborhood was crappy. There were no jobs available and I needed money. Well, shoot I had to have it. The person who wasn't about to stand in the county line waiting for their pennies and food stamps was I.

I started hanging out with the wrong crowd again, which were some gang

members. I dressed like a tomboy, and so I guess that meant I was a target for dikes (bulldaggers). I had some cash, a car, and was always smoking that good herb. I didn't realize what I was setting myself up for. Things were all bad. There was this one particular homegirl that loved her dude, or so I thought. It turned out she would be my first girl. I had a precious son, hadn't finished college, and I was still on a mission. My mom's dude was a trip; living at that house was a no-no for me. This fool smoked crack like there was no tomorrow. It didn't bother me until he started tripping on my mom. She was a dumb ass, and didn't have the guts to make this fool leave, so I had to go. Isn't that the typical needy female? I don't think she'll ever learn. My mom helped me get my place, which was nice. I can't complain.

My son's father was a goofy character. Gucci's his name. He was one of those mixed dudes, and I couldn't resist his fine behind. He kept himself looking older than he really was. I couldn't figure out why his conversation was different than I was used to. It was later, after the baby, when I found out his true age. It was too late for us to undo what we had done. I figured two years younger wouldn't hurt anybody, unless his mom had a problem. It's a good thing she didn't. Gucci was a hustler, and I should have known. Where I'm from, hustlers usually get caught up. It seems as if he was always getting himself into one crime or another. The crimes led his butt to eight years in prison.

I told you about the homegirl I had, who loved her baby's dad. Well, I didn't know she was bisexual. Before my son's father went to jail, he told me to stop hanging out with her because she's a dike. I told him, "Boy she's in love with her dude." He said, "That's not true. Nana could be a down low girl." I hung out with her for over two years. As soon as, Gucci's behind was hauled off to jail, Nana and I were chilling at my crib higher than two dizzy bees. I said, "What type of madness is this?" She said, "Oh, I thought it was cool." I was high tripping.

All I can remember is Nana, short for banana, peeling her clothes off and I saw that entire hairy ol' pussycat. I was still shocked, but also confused as a mermaid. I didn't know what was going on. Then she grabbed me and said, "Here touch this." I was like a kid, knowing that this was so wrong. I just wanted to feel what another girl was all about. How could two of the same sex, have sex? I let my curiosity get the best of me. I kind of liked this strange touching of her pussycat. Shoot, I never touched mine in such a way or caress. It was different in a way, but still the same ol' lips and clit. The time came when my high went down and reality was all around me, my son in the next room and his dad's clothes all over. This broad had to go. I did mean now, and right now. I drove her home and kicked her out my car with a threat of not telling anyone about us or we were done.

I went home and thought how would everyone take this dilemma when they hear about it. I was truly upset, especially at my son's father. He got dragged off to jail, rent had to be paid, and I needed a babysitter. I had to get to work, so I broke down and called what I thought was my BFF. I didn't hear anyone speaking on our little mishap. I suppose she kept her mouth shut, and I could trust her. I asked if she could watch my son. I thought, "Well, Nana is his godmother." She said, "Yeah." I went to work, as usual, but my car broke down. I had no reliable way to and from work. That meant find some help quick or I would lose my spot, my home, and everything I've worked for. The only thing I knew at that time was turning back to my old behaviors and making some fast cash. The biz went well for a few months but then the police rolled up on me asking me questions. I was scared as hell, but somehow managed to talk my way out of jail. It wasn't long after the first encounter that the police came back but didn't want to talk. He was doing some arresting this particular day. I was one of the less fortunate that went down for the count. They didn't find anything on me.

Shortly after I was released, guess who was on the other side of the jail walls waiting for me? The broad I didn't trust being alone with, Nana. Oh, while I was in jail this time, I ran into this man looking dike. She was talking all this stuff about real dikes and fake dikes. I thought, "Really, this is something new." Since I had this encounter with this so-called real dike, I had to ask myself was I a genuine dike, or just pretending. With my type of character, I couldn't pretend. I had to go all the way. I wasn't hooked to anyone. I was free and single. This was something I could do, if I wanted.

The lifestyle I was living didn't make it any better, which was selling drugs and hanging out. Now, having to deal without a spot, a job, or a school to attend, I had no idea what was next in life. I was out of lock up and the broad was waiting for me, like she knew I was going all the way with the female-on-female thing. Well, she was my friend before all the other stuff went down, so I left with her. Our destination was my grandmother's house. My grandmother was just the nicest grandma a human can have. She didn't mind what I did, as long as I was safe, and she had her cup of tea. I expected my mom to be up at my grandma's house, since I told her I was getting out of jail, and she had my son, but she wasn't.

This gave me the opportunity for who, I thought, would become my girl to go in my old bedroom, and touch each other in those private areas. It was kind of cute, sort of like some different kind of affection. Even though my grandmother was watching TV, she still asked me what we were doing back there in that room. I answered and told her nothing. Grandmother knew I have never brought anyone in her house before, and we were making all that noise. She was no fool. I was the fool. I asked the broad, Nana, if it was going to be just us. She started with all this ol' bull mess. I let her know that I was not about to hide who I was. We were either going to kick it, or we could stop playing these games behind closed doors. She made her choice, which was to keep her diking on the down low. It was time for me to find a female that I could enjoy all to myself.

As I left to get me something to eat, I saw this really pretty girl riding around wearing a fur coat. I couldn't tell you if the fur was real or fake. I could tell you she was fly to my

eye. The finest female I saw that wasn't on TV. I knew from that point on that I had to have her in my life. It took some time trying to find her. I even stopped looking. Then one day, I went to grab a bag of smoke and guess what. She was the one who opened the door. I almost turned around and ran. I kept my cool, bought two bags, and left. I didn't have the guts to say anything, plus I had to move slowly. This was my first time approaching someone on this gay tip.

The next day, I had to check her out. I dressed to impress. Went up to the door, and bam! She opened it. I smiled from ear to ear. I didn't forget to talk this time. I asked her what her lovely name was. She was cool; she let me know her name, which was Cherry Drop. I went on and she asked me if I wanted to come in. I smiled some more and stepped inside. There were kids running around, and I figured they were hers. There were men in the dining area talking, and she was doing some girl's hair. We chit chatted. I was just happy to be in her presence. It was like…wow! The questions I asked didn't mean anything to her. She just answered while we smoked.

I thought she could read where I was coming from, but she didn't. The girl whose hair she was doing understood. The girl explained to Cherry Drop how I dug her beauty. I was shy but I agreed. Cherry Drop was like, "Really? I haven't had a girlfriend before. I don't know about this type of lifestyle." My brother had gotten out of jail but I didn't know. It was crazy the way I found out. My mom brought him over to Cherry's house. When he came in he and Cherry went to the back. I thought he must want a large amount, and she had it stashed in the back. We were chilling, Cherry and I, for about a month at this point. Nobody came over and just went to the back. I was wondering what's really up.

They talked or whatever, returned shortly thereafter, and bro tells me bye. I thought, "Okay, what's up with him? He's in a rush like that?" She didn't say anything, nor was she acting the same. She seemed lost. I told her I have to go and she said bye. The next thing I saw was he and her together. I thought, "Hey what's up with that?" I was cool. That's how I should be. I didn't know what was going on. Did she know that's my brother, not just one of my homies? Things weren't looking so bright. I went by Cherry's house to find out what the business was between them. She told me, "He's cool. I guess he likes me." I asked if she knew that he's my blood brother. She said, "Well, I wasn't for sure, but he and I aren't together."

All I could do was believe her word. I hadn't spoken to my brother about it. He didn't know that I was dealing with females. I kind of kept my bedroom life away from my family. Anyway, she and I weren't together yet. She just knew I liked her. I backed off a little, but I still came by every day, and asked her if she needed anything. One day she said, "Yes, could you do a favor for me?" I felt as if she finally noticed me. Now this girl was an eye stopper. I knew I wasn't the only one on her bumper. I had to be original to win her over. To be with a female seemed a bit weird. Well, to me, it was certainly something new. We ended up becoming closer. She let me all the way in her life. I was kicking it every day, getting very personal. I had to take care of my son, plus make some money. I chose the wrong route again, but played it a little safer. I had my car but I liked to take my son on little walks. Every store we needed was within walking distance. Cherry's house was on the same road, which was convenient for me, but not convenient enough for her.

She started liking me a whole heck of a lot. She would leave her two kids at home and come pick up my son and me so we could spend the night. I thought, "This is cool. We're really becoming that couple I wished for." Life was looking up, I thought. As I was cruising the avenue, the cops stopped my car for tinted windows. I was going down because I was on probation. Cherry Drop was upset. I was upset. I explained to her that life must go on. I knew I had to do some time. They were going to send me up the river this time. Cherry and I said our goodbyes. I felt as if I would just drag her down. The best idea I came up with was to let her live her life without worrying about me.

While I was in county, I met this female named Pineapple. She was one of those Hawaiian women. Our relationship was short. She got out of jail, and went back to Hawaii, but not before we took a nice hot shower together. She left happy. She even had someone come visit me and tell me how

BEEN
DETOURED

much she missed me and she would love for me to go back to Hawaii with her. I let her know how awesome that would be, but my son lived here. I would have to pass on that invitation. I loved to see her coming, and also hated when she had to walk away. She had two boys of her own, to whom she had to return to and love.

The county jail was so crappy. Females came in and then you saw them going out. Most of the women there must have had the same charge: being ugly and hanging out beyond the walls of the zoo. Let me tell you, if you had my eyes only for a day, you would rush and give them back. Every blue moon, some broad would come in that was decent-looking. I was on my way to prison any day. I was just waiting for the bus. The day finally came for the long ol' bus ride to the State Prison. I had to go through the motions. First, we stripped together, which I hated. I would never give anyone a sneak peek at this body. You have to be special to see all this.

Next, I was waiting for a bed all damn day! Some wannabe ol' nurse gave me a TB shot. I said, "Broad, I hate shots." I finally received my bed, took a shower, and went straight to sleep. I woke up and went out to the yard to see what this place was all about. I didn't run into any pretty girls. Yes, I received a lot of kites (letters), from these broads that looked like mud ducks. I tore them all to pieces. All the women looked rough. Just when I thought, "Well, I guess I'm going to have to settle for one of these things. A girl needs some company," a cute young lemon-flavored girl came walking in. I was one of the first to see her. I moved quickly toward her, and asked what was up with her, and does she get down with the get down. Her reply was, "Yes, why?" I could tell she was upset about something, and I knew exactly what I had to do. I had to make sure she was all right, then check how much time she had to do, which I found out she lied about. (I'll tell about that part later.) Then, I had to make her smile. Making people smile is my specialty. She ended up hanging with me.

We went over the wall together. "Over the wall" was the programming side. This lemon flavor was right on time. She knew how to braid hair, cook, and have a good time. Her hair was long, and her booty was nice and right. I had to call this one my wife. The wife thing was what we did. Having a wife meant they were going to be together a long time. Plus, I wasn't into sharing. Things about her past started coming to the surface. She couldn't hide certain things anymore. I found out she had a husband. She lied about her time and was running out of excuses. I thought about how everything she told me was a lie. It was cool because she ended up cheating on me and we broke up.

I ended up with a new flavor of fruit that was yum-giving-me-some Coconut. She was good, one of my favorites. I loved everything about her except her feet. It seemed as if she walked from Africa to Alaska. I did my duty, and helped the poor girl. I think that's why she loved me so. I made her feel like she looked super good from head to toe. I knew I had the baddest female on the yard. Well, not like that, because bragging isn't what I do. My motto is one woman at a time, and Coconut kept her attention poured all over. The connection was off the hook. When she wore all white, I swear, you had to see it to believe it. She was a dream come true. I couldn't stop putting one of my fingers in my mouth, with the thought of her replacing it. This female was surely a keeper. When we received our out date, we made plans to hook up and exchange information, and everything. This was going to be my shining star. She got out about a year before me but, as soon as she left, it seemed like she did a damn u-turn and came right back to jail. I knew it was over. Everything we planned was over. (I'm glad I didn't get a tattoo with her name. I would have been looking for her butt, just to tell her how wrong she was.)

Things happen for a reason they say. It was my time to go home, and I knew my son was missing his mom. I planned to live righteous this time. I called this dude up from my past, which kept money. It seemed to me he was doing fine. He never went to jail from what I knew. I felt this dude, KJ, must have been doing something legal to get his money. I went to hang out with him, and he showed me what he was up to, which was cashing checks. It was supposed to have been safe, cool, and all that good stuff.

Man, if I tell you it wasn't but 60 days, two good months, I was on the streets just to go right back to prison for a parole

violation. Can you believe it? I sure in the hell couldn't believe it. I felt gravity pulling my son further away from me. This prison term, I went to fire camp, and ran into this Mango-tango type mommy. She was jazzy, loved to dance, smile, and just have herself a merengue of a time. Mango's vibes were just what I needed, since I was so down and out. My feelings needed to be lifted up by a cool chick, such as herself. She was the right one to fix the mood. She liked to party privately, the same kind I liked. Mango stayed in the unit, made tamales, and dolled herself up for the both of us. I enjoyed her company. She was one of those spicy females; she didn't like other females all in my grill. It was one thing she didn't play about. I respected Mango. I felt that we had to meet on common ground because I liked talking to all the nice women. She agreed, and we kept everything peaceful. Then, she was shipped off to camp. I had some more training to do before I was able to leave for the campsite. She would come back to visit me for a short while, until she found someone where she was. I guess we weren't feeling each other that tough, to hold each other down.

Believe me, I did the same thing. This female here was my watermelon-makes-you-scream type of woman. She turned me on with her seductive dancing. Every time she moved, I wanted to move with her. I could tell this was going to be a sweet romance. She wanted me the first time she spotted me. Watermelon told me how she sat back in the cut waiting, and thinking about me all the time. I asked, "Really?" She said, "Hell, yeah, you're so sexy." We actually took the time out to get to know each other, as much as you could in prison. I experienced a whole new world. I didn't know this type of world existed. This world was a world that belongs straight to her. My juicy watermelon took me for a seedless adventure. This little rendezvous went something to this effect: we were in prison so, we don't have long to get our rocks off. Right away, she got in the shower, and we both had on our smell goods. Then, we went to the room. She started directing traffic, like no officer I had ever seen. "Go here, go there, don't stop, don't breathe, yes, yes, right there! You got it now." I thought, "Well, well. This was some hot sweaty 15-minute workout. The best I ever had." Melon hit me in all the right spots. A little whispering in the ear, at just the right time, did justice for the moment. It sent me straight to the top of the world. If I would have known all these sex moves awhile back, I know somebody would have paid for me a good lawyer. That's no joke.

Even though the sex was the bomb, Ms. Melon had serious issues about the length of time she had to do. She had been down over a decade. She wanted to go home, but had more time to do. That's when I had to go to my box of tricks, and pull a rabbit out the hat. I spoke to her from the heart, so that she'd be able to trust me. I treated her as a dear friend. I went home eventually, kept in contact, and sent her things she needed. It was as if I fell under some type of spell, but was glad to be of service. After all, everyone deserves a true friend. A few years went by, and melon was out of prison. We hooked up, went a few places, and had a blast. I made her feel good about herself. She did about 12 years so she didn't have anyone she could trust. We'd even made plans to get a place together. I was ready; she was ready. We felt like this could really work out.

Then smack right in the face, the road hazards of life happened so fast. I forgot to mention, while Melon was inside the walls of prison, I hung with this pal of mine, getting fast money. I must have sold something to the wrong person. There was a Federal case waiting for my behind to slip up and I did. I caught myself up by not paying attention. Out of the sky, it seemed, the Feds arrested me. Just like that, my life on the streets was over. Ms. Melon tried to stay down for me, but she ended up back in jail. We needed each other to be free. She couldn't handle things without me. That's what I believed, but when God's will is done in your life, there is no way of stopping it. Now that's a for sure thing.

I was stuck in the Feds with a 10-year bid. Not knowing how the heck I was going to explain this to my son. I told him all the time, "Son, do good deeds, I love you. Be an honest, hard working person." I'm saying all that, while I was in the worst place on earth.

I was back to my old self and in need of some company. I spotted this little Kiwi, real delicate fruit. I approached her with ease. I didn't want her to turn around and slap me for tapping her on the arm. Kiwi was looking down. I said to myself, "This one might be a challenge. Heck; I'm up for it. I could use a challenge in my life." I felt as if this would be my last rodeo anyway. With Kiwi, I felt she needed a little more than I ever could give her, and I knew a man was all she needed. I asked her some personal questions and she answered them with ease. Days had passed, and we hadn't spoken to each other. I was still trying to find my way around this unfamiliar institution. She found me over near the exercise area. Kiwi couldn't actually get any time alone with me for the simple fact that I was busy. I was thinking about how to take my time with her, because I didn't like to move fast. When I moved too fast, I always ended up crashing. We made plans to get together later that week to spend some quality time. (Remember I'm in the Feds, and there are a lot of crafty minds here, so I stayed on the alert.) As I learned more about how the women moved about, I no longer had to worry. These women here were old-timers; they don't know too much of anything. I thought, "Man I'm with big girls now. This should be fun. My time will go by quickly."

Well, that was a lie. I tricked myself into believing some very untrue stories people told me that never did a day behind bars. This Fed time has been the toughest time I've ever done. The women there played so many games. I had to see if Kiwi was even worth my time. I was trying to feel her out. That didn't last long. I had to see a different side of her…basically, naked. I had a lustful spirit in me, and I wanted it to be released. I released it on her, and she took to it well. She was trying to tell me it was too early, but I told her I'm not going to change. "I'm not the type to try to switch up. I've seen all that I had to choose from. I chose you so don't trip." I didn't even ask her how long she had to do. I just knew how long I had, which was too much time for me.

Our time spent together seemed to be on the mature side. I was glad she had all her marbles. Well, that's what I thought in the beginning. Now, I'm an aggressive female, and sometimes I can get kind of hood. I don't think she understood what I meant. I guess she's from a small town, one damn near in the mountains. One day I told her to shut the hell up, and boy let me tell you. This little Kiwi didn't behave like that sweet girl I met. This was a whole new fruit. It was all right the first time she took off on me, because we talked it over. Another bad convo, and bam, she kicked me. The abuse didn't stop. She had life, and BS twisted. I wish y'all could have seen her. She was no bigger than a fly. I could have taken her head off her body, with two good hits. I had to let her know I'm not the one to be played with like a slinky.

"You need some help. I would like for you to calm down, and go to church with me." This girl had demons in her. It took prayer and God's Angel's to clear, and clean up this child's mind. The way she went off was unlike anything I had ever seen or dealt with. Sour Apple had some anger built up in her. I tried for months to convince her that I was trying to help; I wasn't the enemy. Just as I was getting through to her, guess what she received…her paperwork informing her of her freedom. Praise God. I caught her just in the nick of time. Someone probably would have rung her neck, the way her attitude would get the best of her. In the end, I think she realized how true friends were hard to run across, but she found one in me. I'm glad she was grateful, and continued to stay in contact.

I learned a lesson through all these worldly fruits. The best fruit is the fruit off my own tree. God is the love of my life. I'm going to keep praying for all the lost souls. I know, by-golly, I was one of them. I choose now to help women in a totally different way: by leading them to God's unchanging word. A person changes when they're ready to change and accept God in their lives. He has helped me so much. I can't thank him enough. I can only try by spreading the good news and read his word over and over. Trust me, God knows your intentions. The good deeds we do, count for us in the end. So smile, and think positive thoughts. We want to make all our good deeds outweigh our bad deeds. I don't want to preach to you. I would like if you take some time out, and picture your life without order.

Never give up or stop believing in yourself. This world will beat you down with lies. Don't fall for it. Today and every day is a new day. Find strength in yourself to make your life a life of peace, headed in the right direction. God is Almighty. He has

our back as long as we believe, pray, and treat others as we would like to be treated. Learn from life experiences. Build your mind up on a sure foundation. Trust me; no one on this earth will be able to tear it down. Reach for the ultimate goal: to meet our creator, our Lord, and Teacher. Don't be a fool all your life; some is okay, but not at all. Find that true you that God has intended for the world to see. When will your enough be enough? Mine is now! It's your time to choose. May God be with you.

CPSIA information can be obtained
at www.ICGtesting.com
Printed in the USA
BVHW071009020821
613407BV00001B/163